The Best Me I Can Be

Mercedes Miller

Archway Publishing books may be ordered through booksellers or by contacting:

Archway Publishing
1663 Liberty Drive
Bloomington, IN 47403
www.archwaypublishing.com
844-669-3957

Interior Image Credit: Lucy Shin

Colossians 3: 12-13 of the King James Bible

ISBN: 978-1-6657-2767-9 (sc)
ISBN: 978-1-6657-2768-6 (hc)
ISBN: 978-1-6657-2766-2 (e)

Print information available on the last page.

Archway Publishing rev. date: 07/29/2022

I am brave, I am confident,
I am beautiful.

My name is
Cielo Marie.

I was born a little bit different than everyone you see.

Some people have fair skin and others may have darker skin.

4

I was born
with both.

5

Mama says God created everyone unique and special in their own way.

I just see me as me and sometimes forget that I have spots on my skin.

Sometimes when I go to school or to the store I hear other people talk about the spots on my skin. They sometimes even stare and laugh at me for being different from them.

There are times when I get mad or sad for having different skin. Sometimes I wish I had normal skin like everyone else.

But then I remember
what Mama's always
taught me. She taught
me that I am brave,
confident, and beautiful.

She also taught me that no
two people are the same. And
that God created everyone
to be different and unique.

Just like butterflies, with
different spots and colors on their
wings, each butterfly is different
and unique in their own way.

I guess I am pretty brave and confident after all. Like when I help little Rosie Jay find her way back to mama when she's lost at the store,

13

Or when I stand in front of a crowd during my dance recital.

Although some people may not have nice things to say, Mama also says the Bible talks about loving your enemy and being merciful.

Which means I should
forgive others even when
they are being mean.

16

So the next time I see people stare at me
or make fun of me for being different,
I'm not going to let it bother me. Because
I know I am the best me that I can be.

I know that I will forgive others even when they say mean and hurtful things.

I know that I am
brave, I am confident,
and I am beautiful;

I love being me.

Printed in the United States
by Baker & Taylor Publisher Services